www.davidgoddard.org

Brighton
From the Air

DB
PUBLISHING

Contents

Introduction

This is an aerial journey around the city of Brighton and its outstanding countryside. All the sites included in this book are chosen by the people of Brighton.

Our journey starts over the city centre, looking down at the contrasting buildings, from the formality of Brighton's crescents and squares to the meandering narrow alleyways of its lanes, the Classical Greek style of Brighton Town Hall and the modernist and Art Deco apartment buildings of Hove. Amid the muted colours of the Georgian streets, vibrant thoroughfares can be found such as Sydney Street.

Brighton's industrial past is evident all over the city, in the large monolithic factories of the Oppenheimer Diamond Works and the Allen West Factory on the Lewes Road, and the old Victorian Pumping station on the Droveway.

Tucked away from the main tourist streets are some hidden architectural gems, like the Sassoon Mausoleum in Kemp Town, the Western Pavilion on Western Terrace and the French Convalescent Home on the Kemp Town seafront.

Through the heart of Brighton runs a green slice of formal gardens, fountains and parks, from the Southern Enclosure on Old Steine to the Victoria Gardens, The Level and Park Crescent.

The city's roof lines are among the most varied and individual of any city I have flown over, from the 78ft of the Brighton Dome and the minarets of the Brighton Pavilion to the sweeping, pitched-glass iron roof of Brighton Railway Station.

Flying north-east from Shoreham Harbour the area's diverse Sporting arenas are very evident, including Brighton and Hove Greyhound Staduim on Neville Road, Sussex Cricket Ground in Eaton Road, the 1930s Withdean Stadium and the new football stadium at Falmer.

In every direction there is evidence of Brighton's popularity through its transport links, all seeming to converge on the city's tourist epicenters.

To the east of the city the legacy and sheer ambition of Thomas Read Kemp can be seen through his fashionable Regency-style estates and streets.

Continuing east along the coast, we are faced with the glacier-like cliffs of the Seven Sisters, towering over the English Channel. This definitive end to the South Downs is one of part of the most iconic symbols of our island nation, between Cuckmere Haven and Eastbourne. The natural landscapes around Brighton are truly jaw-dropping, from the spectacular South Downs to the historic flatlands of the High Weald.

The South Downs hide many man-made and geographical treasures, including the Chattri Monument, the motte and bailey fortress of Edburton Castle, the Jack and Jill windmills overlooking Clayton and the ridge section of Ditchling Beacon.

The flatlands of Sussex, north of the Downs, have many resplendent historical houses dating from the 16th century, including Winston House, the 17th-century Streat Place, the Elizabethan manor house of Plumpton Place and Coombe Place near Offingham.

From 2,000ft Brighton does look like a capital city by the sea, with the royal residences, the grand town halls and the formal squares. But from 1,000ft you see the detail, the individuality and even a small-town charm shining through.

I have been travelling to this city by plane, car and bike for many years. Yet the suggestions from the people of Brighton have educated me about a side of this area that I did not even know existed. Thank you, people of Brighton. This truly is a great city.

David Goddard

City Centre

The Royal Pavillion is located between Old Steine and New Road, only 320m from the sea. The Indo-Saracenic palace was designed by John Nash in 1815 and was finished in 1823 for the Prince Regent, later to become King George IV. The building was intended as a venue for large social events and for use as a seaside retreat. Following the death of George IV and William IV, the Royal Pavillion was sold by the then monarch Queen Victoria to the town of Brighton for £50,000.

The North Gate of the Royal Pavillion. This Grade II listed building was built in 1774 .

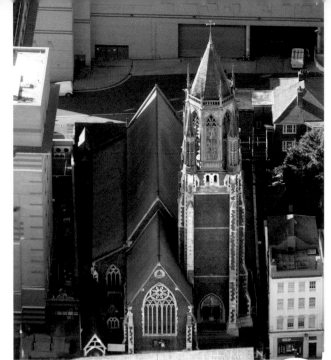

St Paul's Church in Russell Place was built in 1848 in Gothic Revival style. The church features a series of stained-glass windows designed by A.W.N. Pugin.

St Peter's Church was built in 1824–28 in a Perpendicular Gothic style by Charles Barry. The church is located in the centre of Brighton between Richmond Place and York Place.

The Grade II-listed St Nicholas's Church is Brighton's oldest church, the original parts of the building dating back to before the Domesday Book of 1086.

St Mary's Church, on Surrenden Road, Preston Park, was built between 1910 and 1912 in Kentish Ragstone, with Bath stone dressing and a Cornish slate roof.

St Bartholomew's Church, located on Ann Street, was built between 1872 and 1874 by the architect Edmund Scot for the Revd Arthur Douglas Wagner. This 135ft high, Italian Gothic-style place of worship is believed to be the tallest parish church in the UK.

The Town Hall in Bartholomew Square was built in 1830–32 by the town commissioners and designed by Thomas Cooper on the site of the old market. Thomas Read Kemp laid the first foundation stone in April 1830.

London Road Viaduct was built in the 1840s by the railway engineer and architect John Urpeth Rastrick. The Grade II-listed structure is 1200ft long, has 27 arches and contains over 10 million bricks. The Viaduct is located just 300 yards to the north of Brighton Railway Station on the East Coastway Line.

The southern view of Brighton Railway Station's large double-spanned curved glass and iron roof, covering the platforms, which was renovated in 1999 and 2000.

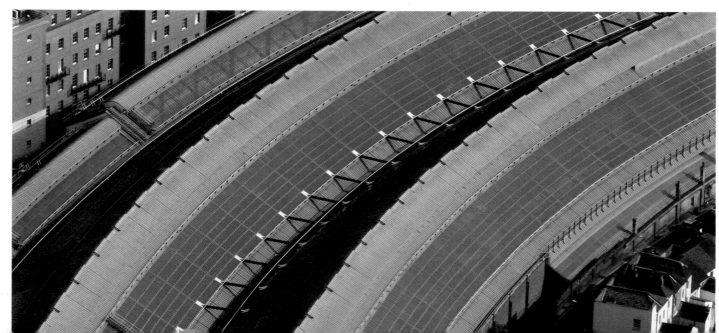

Brighton railway station on Queens Road, which was finished in 1840 by the London & Brighton Railway. The passenger station was designed by David Mocatta in an Italianate style. Over the next 40 years the station was altered and extended due to the growing passenger demand. Today it has been designated as a Grade II-listed building.

Clifton Gardens were built in 1847, at the same time as Clifton Terrace was built. They are located west of Dyke Road and north of Upper North Street.

To the west of The Level and north-east of the city centre is the residential patchwork of Hanover Street, Hanover Terrace, Coleman Street and Washington Street.

Marlborough Place, overlooking Victoria Gardens.

The Salvation Army Brighton Congress Hall on Crescent Terrace, just north of The Level.

Sussex Heights on St Margaret's Place. This 335ft, 26-floor building was built in the late 1960s.

A contemporary apartment building in the New England Quarter.

Brighton's new Materials Recovery Facility on Hollingdean Lane.

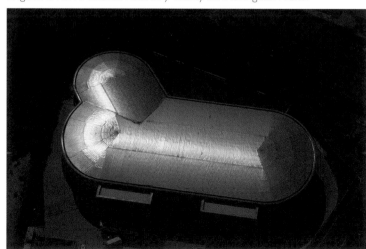

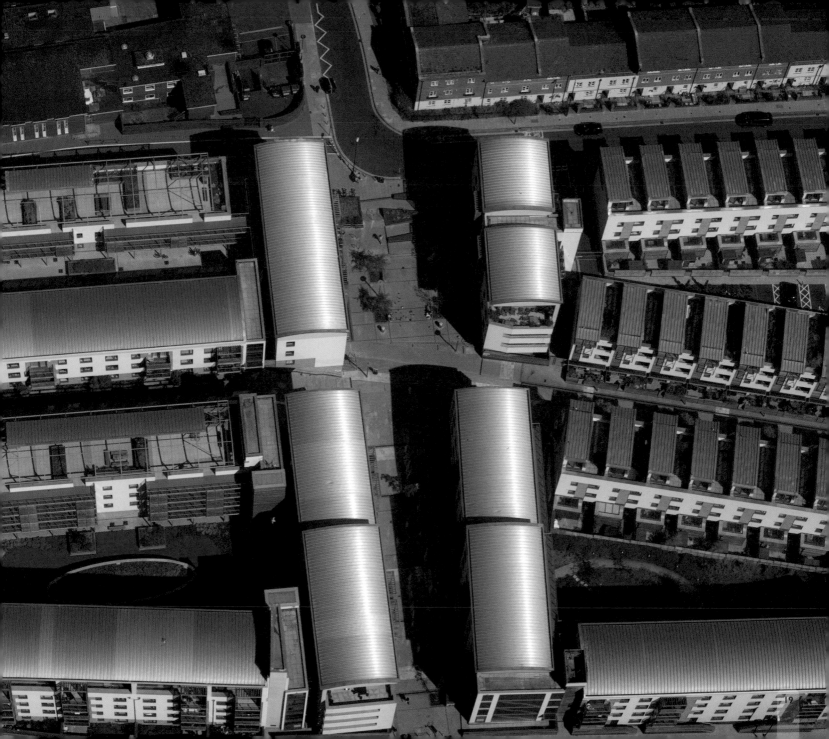

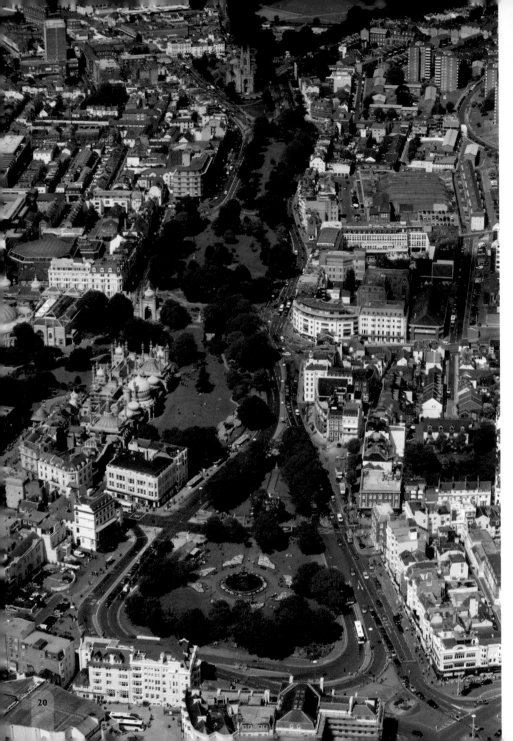

The southern end of Preston Park, including the Rotunda café, the Rose Garden and the other formal gardens.

Opposite:
Park Crescent Terrace is located to the north-east of The Level.

Victoria Fountain, situated in the middle of the southern enclosure, was inaugurated on 25 May 1846 for the Queen's 27th birthday.

The gardens, fountains and parkland that run north through the centre of Brighton from Old Steine, next to the Royal Pavillion to Victoria Gardens and beyond.

The corner of New Road and North Street in the centre of Brighton.

The Grade II-listed terraced houses, retail outlets and offices on the street called Pavilion Buildings, adjacent to the Royal Pavilion, built in 1852–53.

Preston Manor can be found in the north-eastern corner of Preston Park. The present building was built in 1738 by the squire, Thomas Western.

The Duke of York Cinema in Preston Circus, the first purpose-built cinema in Brighton, was constructed in an Edwardian Baroque style and opened on 22 September 1910.

A southern view of the city centre from 4,000ft.

23

The Lanes are a collection of narrow alleyways and lanes dating back to the late 18th century. They are situated to the south of North Street, north of Bartholomew Square and east of Ship Street.

The shopping area of Sydney Street is located between Gloucester Road and Trafalgar Street in the centre of Brighton.

Right: The Lanes offer an eclectic mix of specialist shops, pubs and fashionable resturants. The area was once the centre of the old fishing town.

East Street's junction with North Street. East Street dates back to the 14th century, and today it forms part of the eastern boundary of the Lanes.

Gardner Street in the north Lanes area.

Western Road, situated in the centre of Brighton, has been one of Brighton's main shopping thoroughfares for 100 years. The road's name originates from the local Western family.

Churchill Square Shopping Centre on Western Road was built in the 1960s and then rebuilt in 1998. Today the building covers an area of 500,000sq ft, and comprises 85 shops, three floors and parking for 1,500 cars.

26

Brighton and Hove's
Seafront

King's House on Queen's Gardens. In the past this building was Prince's Hotel and the headquarters of a utility company. In the 1980s the building was extended and refurbished, and today it is the home of Brighton and Hove City Council.

The iconic Grand Hotel on Kings Road was built in 1864 and designed by Victorian architect John Whichcord.

The Metropole Hotel, on Kings Road, is locacted to the west of the Grand Hotel. Brighton's biggest hotel was opened in 1890 and designed by architect Alfred Waterhouse.

King's Gardens are situated on Brighton and Hove's seafront.

An eastern view of Brighton and Hove's seafront and the contrasting buildings of Kingsway and Kings Road, West Pier, Brighton Pier, Brighton Marina and the undulating Seven Sisters at the top.

Charles Street bar and club on Marine Parade, opposite the Sealife Centre.

The Van Alen building on Marine Parade, completed in 2001, was designed by architect P.R.C. Fewster. The building is named after the architect of New York's Chrysler Building, William van Alen.

West Beach Hotel is located on the corner of Kings Road and Preston Street.

Fashionable restaurants on the corner of Kings Road and Regency Square.

A north-western view of the many seafront hotels, apartment buildings and commercial premises located along Kings Road.

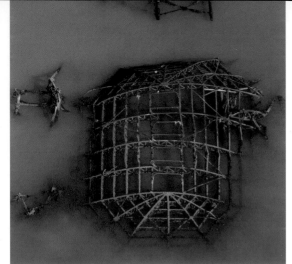

West Pier was built in 1866 and designed by Eugenius Birch. Over the following years six ornamental houses were added, then two toll houses and glass screens. In 1875 a bandstand was added, and in 1880 steamer landing stages and a large pavillion. In 1916 the last building was added to the pier, which was the concert hall.

The West Pier had become one of the best surviving Victorian and Edwardian seaside buildings in the UK. The pier's sad decline started with a violent storm on 28 December 2002 when it partially collapsed, and this was followed by two fires in 2003.

The ruined remains of the West Pier's Pavillion.

A northern view of the ruined West Pier and Regency Square on Brighton's seafront.

Brighton Pier, also known as Palace Pier, was opened in May 1899 at a cost of £137,000. This 1,760ft-long pier was designed by R. St George-Moore. The Palace Pier replaced the original Royal Suspension Chain Pier that was demolished in 1896. In 1901 the pier consisted of dining rooms, smoking rooms, reading rooms and a concert hall. 1911 saw the conversion of the concert hall into a theatre. In 1932 a big wheel was added, and the pier was widened and extended. Following World War Two the popularity of the pier rocketed. Today the pier consists of the Palm Court restaurant, Palace of Fun, arcades, bars and the funfair occupying the end of the pier.

Brighton Pier, also known as Palace Pier, lies south-east of the city centre.

35

The Peace Statue, just off the Kings Road on Hove's seafront. This 30ft-tall memorial to Edward VII, the Peacemaker, was designed by Newbury Trent and unveiled by the Duke of Norfolk in October 1912.

The Milkmaid Pavilion off Kings Road on the very popular Hove seafront.

The Beach Hut Cafe on Kings Road. This old Victorian architectural gem is located opposite West Street between the piers.

A basketball court on the Kings Road Arches.

Brighton's shingle beach, just off Madeira Drive, east of Brighton Pier.

A quayside building and boardwalk overlooking the Marina.

Brighton Marina is located to the east of the city centre. Construction started on this 126-acre marina in 1971 and it was opened by Queen Elizabeth II in 1978. The construction and development of the rest of the complex continued for the next 27 years, resulting in the biggest marina complex in Europe, with 863 residential properties and many varied leisure and retail outlets.

The eastern end of the Marina, which has berths for 1,600 yachts.

The Brighton Bandstand, also known as the Birdcage, is located on Kings Road, south of Bedford Square. It was designed by Phillip Causton Lockwood in 1883 and constructed in 1884 by Walter Macfarlane & Co. of Saracen Foundry in Glasgow.

A northern aerial view of Brighton's Old Town and seafront. The Old Town has the boundary of East Street, North Street, West Street and the seafront. The area dates back to the 14th century and is regarded as the historic heart of Brighton.

The eastern edge of the Brighton Marina and the chalk cliffs below Roedean.

A yacht sailing west between the Palace Pier and Brighton Marina.

The dredger *Split Three*, dredging the channels in and around the Brighton Marina.

The beach volleyball courts on Madeira Drive opposite the Volks Railway.

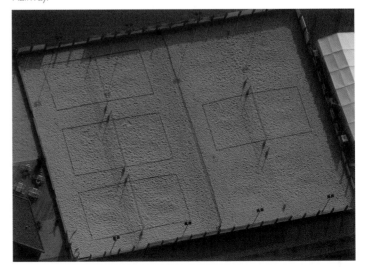

The three man-made structures that protrude into the English Channel from Brighton's seafront: West Pier, Brighton Pier and Brighton's Marina.

West

Brighton and Hove

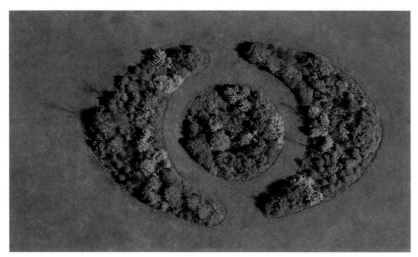

The eye-shaped garden at the northern end of Brunswick Square.

Brunswick Square, off Kingsway in Hove. This Grade I-listed square was built in the 1820s and was one of Hove's first housing developments.

The western side of Brunswick Square.

Sussex County Cricket Ground on Eaton Road in the centre of Hove, one mile north-west of Brighton city centre.

The Art Deco building on Princess Crescent and Kingsway, built in 1931, was designed by the architect Robert Cromie for Ian Stuart Miller, the film director and tycoon.

Brighton & Hove Greyhound Stadium in Nevill Road, Hove. Today it is owned by the Gala Coral Group. It is one of the country's leading greyhound stadiums. In July 1962 Queen Elizabeth II visited the track. It holds the world speed record for a greyhound over a 563-yard race track at an average 38.89 mph, which was set on 4 May 1982 by 'Glen Miner'.

King's Gardens on Kingsway between Fourth Avenue and Third Avenue.

The Grade II-listed terminal building at Shoreham Airport. Opened on 13 June 1936, it is situated on the southern side of the airfield.

Shoreham Airport is located seven miles to the west of Brighton city centre, on the west bank of the River Adur. The aerodrome was officially opened in June 1911, and the terminal building was opened in June 1936 and is now a Grade II-listed building.

A Cessna 172 over the threshold on Runway 20 at Shoreham Airport.

The steam tug *Challenge* is situated in Shoreham Harbour. This historic vessel was built in 1931 by Alexander Hall and Co. Ltd, Aberdeen.

Lady Bee Marina, situated just inside the Shoreham Port's main shipping canal.

An eastern view of Shoreham Beach, Kingston-by-Sea and Southwick.

Shoreham Harbour's Prince George Lock, port control and the dry dock.

The Middle Pier in Shoreham Habour.

The eastern side of Shoreham Harbour and the mouth of the River Adur, located three miles to the west of Brighton city centre.

Shoreham Power Station on the southern side of Shoreham Harbour. This new gas-fired power station was opened in 2002 and cost £150 million.

Weald Avenue allotment is one of the biggest sites in the Brighton and Hove area. It is located north of Old Shoreham Road and south of Nevill Avenue.

The Adur River with Shoreham-by-Sea to the north (right) and Shoreham Beach (left).

British Engineerium, a fully-restored working Victorian pumping station and museum, is located on The Droveway, two miles north-east of Brighton city centre.

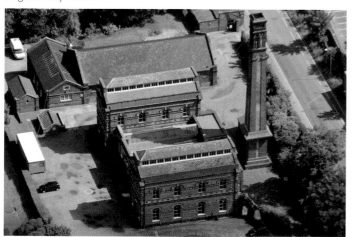

Embassy Court on the corner of Kings Road and Western Street. This Grade II-listed building was designed by Wells Coates and completed in 1935.

St Mary de Haura Church on Church Street in Shoreham. This Grade I-listed Anglican church was built at the end of the 11th century.

The mouth of the River Adur and the entrance to the Shoreham Port. The West Breakwater and the East Breakwater extend out into the English Channel in the foreground, while inland is the small town of Southwick.

St Barnabas's Church, on Sackville Road in Hove, was built in 1882–83.

All Saints' Anglican Church on the corner of Eaton Road and The Drive, Hove. This Grade I-listed building has served this area of Hove since 1891.

The River Adur meandering towards the English Channel, passing the towns of Shoreham-by-Sea and Lancing.

Hove Park, north of Old Shoreham Road and west of Goldstone Cresent, is one of Hove's largest parks. It was created in 1906.

St Andrew's Church in Church Road, Hove, also known as St Andrew (Old Church). Some of the original features of the first Norman-style church date back to the 13th century. St Andrew's was reopened on 18 June 1836.

St Leonard's Church is situated on New Church Road, Aldrington.

The residential steeets of Hove and Portslade. The Port of Shoreham is visible in the distance.

The shops and road junction of New Church Road, Francklin Road and Boundary Road. Boundary Road forms the border between Portslade and Hove.

Vale Park in Portslade is located between St Andrew's Road to the south and Vale Road to the north.

A northern view of Hove Town Hall on Norton Road, which was designed by architect John Wells-Thorpe in 1974.

Lancing College to the west of the River Adur on Lancing Hill, seven miles west of Brighton. This co-educational English independent school was founded in 1848 by Nathaniel Woodard.

Hove Museum and Art Gallery on New Church Road. The museum is based in the former Brooker Hall, designed by architect Thomas Lainson and built for John Oliver Vallance.

St John the Baptist's Anglican Church on Church Road in Hove, which was built between 1852 and 1854.

Western Road, Brighton, running into Church Road through Hove and into New Church Road, ending up in Portslade.

St Peter's Roman Catholic Church on Portland Road was built between 1912 and 1915.

East

Brighton and Hove

The area east of the city centre includes the main East-West roads of Madeira Drive, Marine Parade, St James Street and Edward Street.

The palatial Sussex Square and Lewes Crescent were part of Thomas Read Kemp's big vision to develop the area into a fashionable Regency-style estate. He commissioned two of the most respected architects and builders of their time, Amon Wilds and Charles Busby. The project started in 1823 and was finished in 1855, but resulted in the financial ruin of Thomas Kemp. Thomas Cubitt finished the development. Today the area is known as Kemp Town.

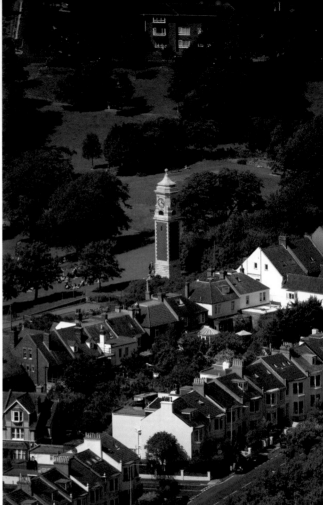

The Grade II-listed clock tower located in Queen's Park was designed by William Godleye in 1915.

Roedean Independent Girls' School is situated two and a half miles to the east of Brighton. The school was founded in 1885 by three sisters, Penelope, Millicent and Dorothy Lawrence, at Wimbledon House. In 1898 architect John William Simpson designed the new school buildings at its present site.

Queen's Park is set in the old Victorian pleasure garden known as Brighton Park, part of a shielded valley to the north of Kemp Town. It was first opened to the public in August 1892 and was renamed in honour of Queen Adelaide. Today it is a very popular park, with tennis courts, playgrounds, wildlife gardens, a lake and scented gardens.

To the east of Brighton overlooking the Marina is the iconic 1930s Marine Gate, a block of 132 purpose-built luxury flats.

Madeira Drive, Marine Parade and Portland Place are located to the east of the city centre.

The old Sassoon Mausoleum, situated on the corner of St Georges Road and Paston Place, is the original grave of baronet Sir Albert Abdullah David Sassoon, the British Indian philanthropist and merchant. It was also the burial site for many other distinguished family members until 1933, when all the remains were moved to Willesden Jewish Cemetery in London. Following World War Two the site was sold and used by many different public houses and night clubs.

Eastern Terrace on Marine Parade, built in 1828, is situated one mile to the south-east of Brighton city centre.

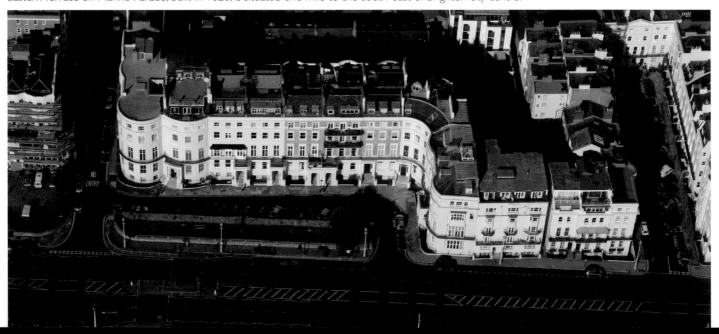

To the east of the city on the seafront is the Grade I-listed Chichester terrace, built in the 1820s using the combined architectural services of Amon Wilds and Charles Busby. The development was finished by Thomas Cubitt.

Royal Crescent on Marine Parade, Brighton's first major development, was built between 1798 and 1807 by the West Indian merchant J.B Otto.

Beacon Mill, also known as Rottingdean Windmill, on Beacon Hill, can be found just to the west of Rottingdean overlooking the south coast. This Grade II-listed smock mill was built in 1802 on the site of an earlier mill.

A south-western view of Woodingdean from above Bullock Hill. This suburb of the city of Brighton and Hove expanded greatly following World War One. Much of the development took place in the 1950s and 1960s.

Saltdean Lido was built in 1937–38 in an Art Deco style by architect R.W.H. Jones. This Grade II-listed building was fully restored at a cost of £2 million and reopened in 1998.

Saltdean is situated on the south coast, four miles south-east of Brighton. Prior to 1920 this area was almost uninhabited. Over the following years Charles W. Neville helped to build Saltdean into a prosperous village suburb of the city of Brighton and Hove.

Grand Crescent and The Park on the western side of Saltdean.

In the village of Rottingdean next to St Mary's Church is The Elms, once home to the British author and poet Rudyard Kipling. He lived at The Elms from 1897 until 1902.

Rottingdean is an historical village less than four miles to the east of Brighton. Over the past 90 years it has seen the creation and dramatic expansion of its neighbouring suburbs, Saltdean and Ovingdean. In the centre of the village is the 13th-century church of St Margaret.

The Rottingdean Road junction of Marine Drive and the southern end of the High Street by the White Horse bar and restaurant.

A north-western view of north Saltdean and Rottingdean.

The southern end of the village of Rottingdean, also Beacon Mill windmill and the Rottingdean Gap, the site of the old Pier, which was built to support Magnus Volk's tram-like boat, originally designed to carry 150 passengers to Brighton. The venture met its end five days after its launch due to a storm in 1896.

St Dunstan's National Centre, located to the south of Ovingdean. Founded in 1915, St Dunstan's is a national charity providing lifelong support and rehabilitation to blind ex-service men and women.

Ovingdean Hall is a School for Deaf Children. It moved to Ovingdean in 1945 from central Brighton, the original school being first established in 1841 by two teachers in Kemp Town. Ovingdean House was first built in 1792 by the Kemp family and many generations of the family lived at the property, but in 1891 it became a school and was renamed Ovingdean Hall. The Kemp family were the founders of Kemp Town.

Royal Sussex County Hospital on Eastern Road, east of the city centre. The main building was designed by Charles Barry and opened on 11 June 1828. Further additions included the Jubilee Building in 1887, the Millennium Building in 2000 and the Audrey Emerton Building in 2005.

The French Convalescent Home on De Courcel Road was opened in 1896 to take convalescents from the French Hospital in Shaftesbury Avenue, London. Today this Grade II-listed building is divided into apartments.

The Church of St George the Martyr, on Abbey Road and St George's Road, was built and completed in 1825 by architect Charles Busby. It was originally constructed to complement the new development of Kemp Town for Thomas Read Kemp.

Marine Square was built in 1825–28 for Thomas Attree by C.A. Busby and Amon Wilds. It is located between Portland and Bloomsbury Place on the seafront.

An eastern view of the coastline from Rottingdean to Saltdean, Peacehaven and Newhaven.

Ovingdean is a village located three miles to the east of Brighton and north-west of Rottingdean. Records show that the village has existed since Anglo-Saxon times. The village saw much expansion following World War One and Two, like its neighbouring villages. Today it has a population of over 1,200.

North
Brighton and Hove

The Patcham Windmill is located on the western side of Coney Hill, two and a half miles to the north-west of Brighton city centre. It was built in 1885 for the baker Joseph Harris.

The A27 dual carriageway to the north of Patcham.

A combine harvester, harvesting the wheat crop in the fields south of Falmer in north-east Brighton.

The Cockcroft Building, Aldrich Library and Watts Building on Lewes Road, which are part of Brighton University's Moulsecoomb campus.

One of the 1950s factory buildings in the Hollingbury Industrial Estate designed by the London architects Townsend.

Hollingbury Industrial Estate, south of the A27 and three miles to the north-east of Brighton city centre. The estate consists of 18 acres of factories, retail outlets and offices. The site was developed by the local authority in the 1950s.

The old Bernard Oppenheimer Diamond Works factory at the junction of Coombe Road and Lewes Road, which was built in 1918.

A western view of the A27, East and North Moulsecoomb, Coldean Hollingbury and the South Downs in the distance.

Mithras House in Moulsecoomb, part of the University of Brighton, was originally the Allen West factory and was built in 1939. In 1977 it became one of the main Brighton Polytechnic buildings.

A south-western view of the Foredown Tower, with the camera obscura looking towards Shoreham Power Station.

Foredown Tower in Portslade Village, the home of the camera obscura, one of only two operational in the south of England. This former water tower was built in 1909.

Withdean Stadium, built in 1936 in the natural amphitheatre of the South Downs, one and a half miles to the north of the city, in the suburb of Withdean. This athletics staduim was once a respected tennis centre, hosting a Davis Cup match between Great Britain and New Zealand in 1939. The site also included a zoo and a miniature railway. In 1952 the city council converted the area into an athletics arena. Today it is a temporary stadium for Brighton and Hove Football Club, until the new stadium is finished at Falmer.

Hollingdean Depot on Upper Hollingdean Road in north Brighton.

Park Village, a hall of residence for undergraduates and postgraduates of the University of Sussex.

The University of Sussex at Falmer. The campus is set amid the South Downs, three and a half miles to the north-east of Brighton. Founded in the 1960s, the University of Sussex received its Royal Charter in 1961. It has since become a leading teaching and research institution.

The Attenborough Centre was built within the boundaries of the University of Sussex. The original 1960s building was called the Gardner Centre.

The sweeping avenues of south Bevendean.

The residential streets of Woodland Drive, Deanway, Downside and Hill Brow in northern Hove.

Ditchling road bridge over the A27 to the north of Brighton.

The railway tunnel under Coney Hill and the Patcham Place estate was built in 1840–41 by the engineer John Urpeth Rastrick.

The hillside residential roads of Moulsecoomb and Bevendean, including The Avenue, Hillside, Heath Hill Avenue and the elliptically-shaped Plymouth Avenue.

Percy and Wagner Alms Houses on Lewes Road. The first six houses were built in 1795 by Mrs Margaret Marriot. A further six almshouses were built in 1859. The houses were originally built for poor widows and poor maidens.

Withdean Park to the south of Patcham. This 38-acre park is regarded as one of Brighton's most beautiful green spaces. It was acquired in 1933 by the Corporation to prevent development on this green space, led by Sir Herbert Carden. The park has the second largest collection of lilacs in the world. Within the park is the site of the old Manor House, believed to have been given to Anne of Cleves in 1541 by Henry VIII.

Stanmer House, north of the great wood in Stanmer Park. This Grade I-listed mansion was constructed by the French architect Nicholas Dubois in 1722.

Stanmer Park is a huge landscaped park, three miles to the north-east of Brighton. Within the park are Stanmer village, Stanmer Church and Stanmer House. Brighton's council bought the park in 1947. Today the once private park is open to the public, and English Heritage gave the park and gardens Grade II-listed status and declared it an area of Special Historic Interest.

Stanmer Church in Stanmer Park, a Grade II-listed building, was built on the site of an earlier church dating from the 14th century. The new church was built in around 1840 by the the 3rd Earl of Chichester, Henry Thomas Pelham.

The Countryside

Plumpton Place is an Elizabethan manor house located to the north of the South Downs and six miles north-east of Brighton. The north wing of the house dates back to 1568, and the landscaping is attributed to Lutyens and Jekyll.

Plumpton Racecourse is situated south of Plumpton Green and 7.5 miles north-east of Brighton. This National Hunt racecourse is a tight left-handed circuit of just over a mile, which held its first race meeting on 11 February 1884.

Streat Place is a manor house on the westen side of the village of Streat, in the shadow of the South Downs. It was built in the early 17th century by Walter Dobell.

Brack Mount is an artificial mound to the north-east of Lewes Castle, between Mount Place and Precincts Castle. It is believed to be a motte, of a motte and bailey castle, constructed after the Norman invasion.

Lewes Crown Court on the High Street in Lewes, built in 1821. This crown court is a high-profile court, able to take all Class 1 cases from East and West Sussex and some High Court civil cases.

The East Sussex county town of Lewes, located on the River Ouse between Offham Hill and Malling Hill, seven miles to the north-east of Brighton, has a rich, colourful recorded history dating back 2,000 years. One of the bloodiest events was the Battle of Lewes between the forces of Henry III and Simon de Montfort, part of the Second Barons' War in 1264. The main battle took place to the north-west of the town.

The High Street in Lewes.

Lewes Castle is in the centre of Lewes, overlooking the surounding roads of West Gate Street, New Road and the High Street. The castle dates from the end of the 11th century. It has just been refurbished, courtesy of the Heritage Lottery Fund.

Ditchling Beacon, 814ft high, is the third-highest point in the South Downs. This domineering grass-covered hill overlooks the village of Ditchling and the flat lands of the Lower Weald to the north.

Edburton Castle is a motte and bailey fortress on the northern edge of the South Downs, six miles north-west of Brighton.

An archaeological dig near Barcombe, north of Lewes.

An archaeological excavation of a Roman villa complex outside the village of Barcombe in East Sussex.

One of the many World War Two bomb craters that litter the countryside around Brighton. This crater is located on the South Downs, west of the Chattri War Memorial.

The northern entrance of Clayton Tunnel, west of the village of Clayton and located 4.7 miles north of the Brighton Railway Station. On the main London to Brighton line, it was built in the 1840s at a cost of £90,000. The tunnel measures 1.25 miles.

The South Downs, seen from 900ft above the village of Ditchling.

Chattri War Memorial is located on the eastern side of Holt Hill, four miles to the north-west of Brighton. This Grade II-listed monument was designed by E.C. Henriques and opened on 1 February 1921 by Edward, Prince of Wales.

Barcombe Cross is a small hamlet in East Sussex, three miles north of Lewes and north-west of the River Ouse.

Fulking is a small West Sussex village in the shadow of the South Downs, six miles to the north-east of Brighton.

The small village of Offham, just to the north of Lewes. The village was settled in 1348 when the Black Death forced the inhabitants to move away from the settlement of Hamsey and the church. For centuries the village was a farming community, which also produced lime and chalk from the quarry on Offham Hill.

Wiston House is a Grade I-listed building located to the north-west of Steyning. It was built in about 1576 by Sir Thomas Shirley. Much of the original house was demolished between 1780 and 1830. Today it is also known as Wilton Park European Discussion Centre.

The town of Burgess Hill, nine miles to the north of Brighton, in the mid-Sussex district of West Sussex. The town is situated in beautiful countryside, with the South Downs to the south and the High Weald to the north.

Coombe Place, to the west of Offham, two miles north-west of Lewes. This Grade II-listed house dates from 1657, when it was rebuilt by Richard Bridger. It was refaced in 1730 by Sir John Bridger.

The western side of Burgess Hill.

Beacon Road climbing up the 787ft of Ditchling Beacon on the northern hillside of the South Downs.

The village of Ditchling in the shadow of the South Downs, six miles to the north of Brighton.

Newhaven is a town located at the mouth of the River Ouse between Peacehaven and Seaford on the south coast. The existence of a village on this site can be traced back to AD 480, with the Saxon name of Meeching. On Castle Hill to the south-west of the town traces of a Bronze Age fort can be found. Today Newhaven is a thriving small port town with an active fishing fleet, marina and an international ferry service.

In the south-western corner of Seaford Bay, at the end of the harbour breakwater, is the much photographed lighthouse. The original lighthouse was built in 1885 but suffered structural damage in 1976, when the building was replaced. The original top section was saved and now can be seen in Paradise Gardens.

A north-eastern view of the Seven Sisters from 750ft, with Seaford Haven in the foreground and West Brow in the distance. These eroding chalk cliffs between Seaford and Eastbourne form the south-eastern edge of the South Downs.

An eastern view of the Seven Sisters from Belle Tout to Beachy Head, including the Belle Tout Lighthouse, Shooters Bottom and the Beachy Head Light House.

The disused chalk quarry on Offham Hill overlooking the town of Lewes and the Ouse Valley.

The South Down's mounds and earthworks, south-west of Ditchling between Clayton Holt and Coombe Bottom.

The Clayton windmills, five miles to the north of Brighton, on the South Downs overlooking the village of Clayton to the north. These Grade II-listed buildings are also known as Jack and Jill. Jill, a post mill, was built in 1821 and Jack, a corn mill, was built in 1866.

The large seaside town of Worthing on the south coast, 10 miles to the west of Brighton. Worthing is a fine example of a Georgian seaside resort. In the surrounding countryside it has the highest concentration of Stone Age flint mines in Britain.

The eastern edge of Sompting and Lancing village, located between Worthing and Shoreham-by-Sea, eight miles to the west of Brighton.